This journal belongs to

....

A Teacher's Journal
© 2009 Ellie Claire Gift & Paper Corp.
WWW.ELLIECLAIRE.COM

Compiled by Barbara Farmer
Designed by Franke Design, Minneapolis, MN

Scripture references are from the following sources: The Holy Bible, New International
Version® NIV®. © 1973, 1978, 1984 by International Bible Society. Used by permission of
Zondervan. The New King James Version (NKJV). Copyright © 1982 by Thomas Nelson, Inc.
Used by permission. The Holy Bible, New Living Translation® (NLT). Copyright © 1996, 2004.
Used by permission of Tyndale House Publishers, Inc., Wheaton, Illinois. The Message © 1993,
1994, 1995, 1996, 2000, 2001, 2002. Used by permission of NavPress, Colorado Springs, CO.
The New Century Version® (NCV). Copyright © 1987, 1988, 1991 by Thomas Nelson, Inc. Used
by permission. The Living Bible (TLB) copyright © 1971. Used by permission of Tyndale House
Publishers, Inc., Carol Stream, Illinois 60188. All rights reserved.

ISBN 978-1-934770-72-6

Printed in China

A TEACHER'S JOURNAL

The best way to lead
is by a good example.

...inspired by life

There is no satisfaction in the world that can compare with seeing the light of understanding in a child's eyes.

MARGARET PERRY TEUFEL

Through wisdom a house is built, and by understanding it is established;
by knowledge the rooms are filled with all precious and pleasant riches.
A wise man is strong, yes, a man of knowledge increases strength.

PROVERBS 24:3-5 NKJV

The most important function of education at any level is to develop the personality of the individual and the significance of his life to himself and to others. This is the basic architecture of a life.

GRAYSON KIRK

*G*etting wisdom is the wisest thing you can do!
And whatever else you do, develop good judgment.

PROVERBS 4:7 NLT

I think of you not only as a teacher,
but as a role model, mentor, leader, guide, and friend.
Thank you for being all those things and more.

Teach the wise, and they will become even wiser;
teach good people, and they will learn even more.

PROVERBS 9:9 NCV

God sends children to enlarge our hearts and to make us unselfish and full of kindly sympathies and affections.

MARY HOWITT

The wisdom from above is first of all pure. It is also peace loving, gentle at all times, and willing to yield to others. It is full of mercy and good deeds. It shows no favoritism and is always sincere.

JAMES 3:17 NLT

*Perhaps the most valuable result of all education
is the ability to make yourself do the thing you have to do,
when it ought to be done, whether you like it or not.*

WALTER BAGEHOT

*L*et no debt remain outstanding, except the continuing debt
to love one another, for he who loves his fellowman has fulfilled the law.

ROMANS 13:8 NIV

Life is no brief candle to me. It is a...splendid torch...
and I want to make it burn as brightly as possible
before handing it over to future generations.

GEORGE BERNARD SHAW

*Y*ou are a chosen generation, a royal priesthood, a holy nation,
His own special people, that you may proclaim the praises
of Him who called you out of darkness into His marvelous light.

1 PETER 2:9 NKJV

If a child is to keep his inborn sense of wonder...he needs the companionship of at least one adult who can share it, rediscovering with him the joy, excitement, and mystery of the world we live in.

RACHEL CARSON

*W*hat a wildly wonderful world, God! You made it all, with Wisdom at Your side, made earth overflow with Your wonderful creations.

PSALM 104:24 THE MESSAGE

When you stood in front of our class, I could see that you
not only cared about us, but you cared deeply about
what you were communicating, and it was contagious.
Thank you for teaching with passion.

This most generous God...gives you something you can then give away, which grows into full-formed lives, robust in God, wealthy in every way, so that you can be generous in every way, producing with us great praise to God.

2 CORINTHIANS 9:10-11 THE MESSAGE

Excellence is a better teacher than mediocrity. The lessons of the ordinary are everywhere. Truly profound and original insights are to be found only in studying the exemplary.

WARREN G. BENNIS

$\mathcal{L}$isten, for I will speak of excellent things, and from the opening
of my lips will come right things; for my mouth will speak truth.

PROVERBS 8:6-7 NKJV

*W*e think of the effective teachers we have
had over the years with a sense of recognition,
but those who have touched our humanity
we remember with a deep sense of gratitude.

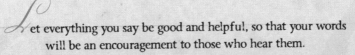

*L*et everything you say be good and helpful, so that your words will be an encouragement to those who hear them.

EPHESIANS 4:29 NLT

I nspiring students with a sense of their own worth gives them the confidence to express themselves more freely, to explore and learn through their mistakes, and to regard learning as an adventure.

JAY SOMMER

Let my teaching fall on you like rain; let my speech settle like dew.
Let my words fall like rain on tender grass, like gentle showers on young plants.

DEUTERONOMY 32:2 NLT

*I*f kids come to us [teachers] from strong,
healthy functioning families, it makes our job easier.
If they do not come to us from strong,
healthy, functioning families, it makes our job more important.

BARBARA COLOROSO

*W*hoever accepts this child as if the child were Me, accepts Me....
And whoever accepts Me, accepts the One who sent Me. You become great
by accepting, not asserting. Your spirit, not your size, makes the difference.

LUKE 9:48 THE MESSAGE

Loving a child doesn't mean giving in to all his whims;
to love him is to bring out the best in him,
to teach him to love what is difficult.

NADIA BOULANGER

*W*e do not enjoy being disciplined. It is painful at the time, but later, after we have learned from it, we have peace, because we start living in the right way.

HEBREWS 12:11 NCV

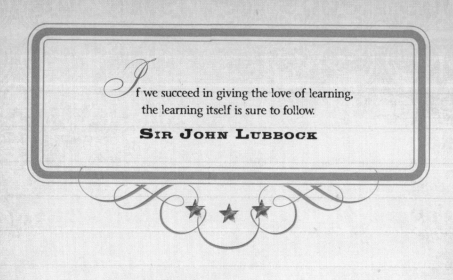

If we succeed in giving the love of learning,
the learning itself is sure to follow.

SIR JOHN LUBBOCK

Those who get wisdom do themselves a favor,
and those who love learning will succeed.

PROVERBS 19:8 NCV

Our heritage and ideals, our code and standards—
the things we live by and teach our children—are preserved or
diminished by how freely we exchange ideas and feelings.

WALT DISNEY

These words which I command you today shall be in your heart.
You shall teach them diligently to your children, and shall talk of them
when you sit in your house, when you walk by the way,
when you lie down, and when you rise up.

DEUTERONOMY 6:6-7 NKJV

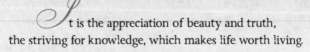

It is the appreciation of beauty and truth,
the striving for knowledge, which makes life worth living.

MORRIS RAPHAEL COHEN

$\mathcal{L}$ove and Truth meet in the street, Right Living and Whole Living
embrace and kiss! Truth sprouts green from the ground, Right Living
pours down from the skies! Oh yes! God gives Goodness and Beauty;
our land responds with Bounty and Blessing.

PSALM 85:10-12 THE MESSAGE

No teacher can expect to be all things to all students. But when you give it your all, you make a difference you can't always see on the surface of their lives.

This is a large work I've called you into, but don't be overwhelmed by it. It's best to start small. Give a cool cup of water to someone who is thirsty, for instance. The smallest act of giving or receiving makes you a true apprentice.

MATTHEW 10:41-42 THE MESSAGE

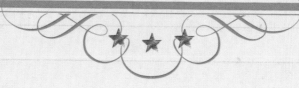

*I*f a child lives with encouragement, he learns to appreciate.
If a child lives with fairness, he learns justice. If a child lives
with security, he learns to have faith.

DOROTHY LAW NOLTE

May God who gives patience, steadiness, and encouragement help you to live in complete harmony with each other.

ROMANS 15:5 TLB

You're my hero! I will always be thankful to you, my teacher, for all the hard work and effort you have invested in my education.

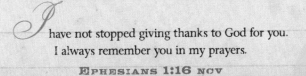

I have not stopped giving thanks to God for you.
I always remember you in my prayers.

EPHESIANS 1:16 NCV

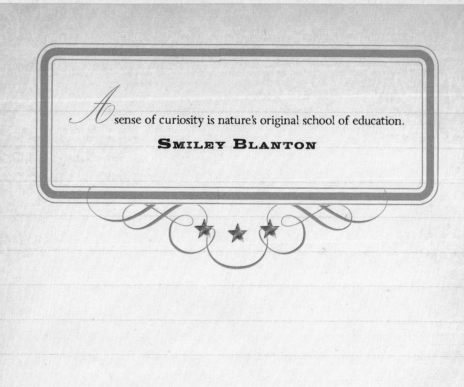

A sense of curiosity is nature's original school of education.

SMILEY BLANTON

Show me Your ways, O Lord; teach me Your paths.
Lead me in Your truth and teach me.

PSALM 25:4-5 NKJV

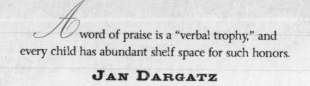

A word of praise is a "verbal trophy," and every child has abundant shelf space for such honors.

JAN DARGATZ

He took the children in His arms,
put His hands on them and blessed them.

MARK 10:16 NIV

My first precept about teaching is to accept every child entrusted to me because each one is his parents' greatest gift. It is my job to accept him as he is, teach him what I must, and help him reach a new and better understanding of himself and the world in which he lives.

MARY V. BICOUVARIS

Children are a gift from the Lord; they are a reward from Him.

PSALM 127:3 NLT

You can teach a student a lesson for a day;
but if you can teach him to learn by creating curiosity,
he will continue the learning process as long as he lives.

CLAY P. BEDFORD

Keep my message in plain view at all times. Concentrate! Learn it by heart! Those who discover these words live, really live; body and soul, they're bursting with health.

PROVERBS 4:21-22 THE MESSAGE

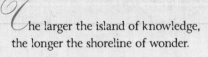

The larger the island of knowledge,
the longer the shoreline of wonder.

RALPH W. SOCKMAN

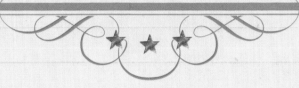

*K*eep your eyes open for God, watch for His works; be alert
for signs of His presence. Remember the world of wonders He has made.

PSALM 105:4-5 THE MESSAGE

The suspense of curiosity is one of the gems of the classroom. The second is the satisfaction of a young mind coming into a discovery.

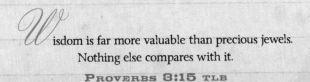

*isdom is far more valuable than precious jewels.
Nothing else compares with it.*

PROVERBS 3:15 TLB

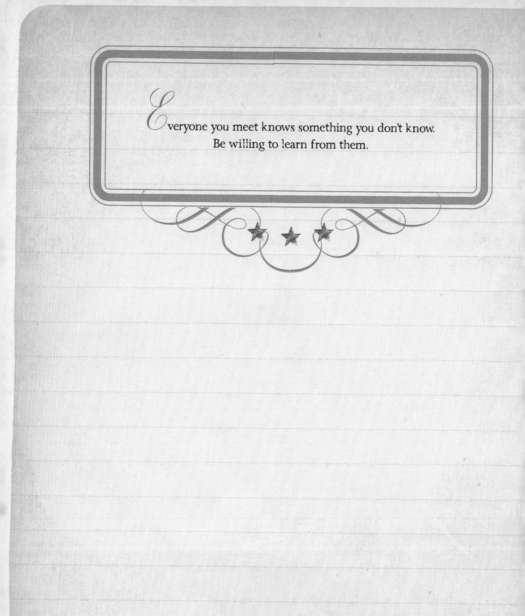

Everyone you meet knows something you don't know.
Be willing to learn from them.

*L*et the teaching of Christ live in you richly. Use all wisdom to teach
and instruct each other by singing psalms, hymns,
and spiritual songs with thankfulness in your hearts to God.

COLOSSIANS 3:16 NCV

To reach a child's mind a teacher must capture his heart.
Only if a child feels right can he think right.

HAIM G. GINOTT

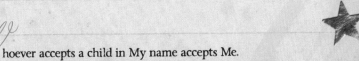
Whoever accepts a child in My name accepts Me.

MATTHEW 18:5 NCV

What other profession offers one the satisfaction of knowing you have lit a spark in the mind of the next generation and nurtured a fire that will burn long after you've gone?

RAE ELLEN MCKEE

*W*e will not hide these truths from our children;
we will tell the next generation about the glorious deeds
of the Lord, about His power and His mighty wonders.

PSALM 78:4 NLT

*I*f you can help anybody even a little, be glad;
up the steps of usefulness and kindness,
God will lead you on to happiness and friendship.

MALTBIE D. BABCOCK

*W*e are not saying that we can do this work ourselves.
It is God who makes us able to do all that we do.

2 CORINTHIANS 3:5 NCV

He who helps a child helps humanity with an immediateness which no other help given to human creatures in any other stage of human life can possibly equal.

PHILLIPS BROOKS

*A*ny of you who welcomes a little child like this because you are Mine is welcoming Me.... Don't look down upon a single one of these little children. For I tell you that in heaven their angels have constant access to My Father.

MATTHEW 18:5, 10 TLB

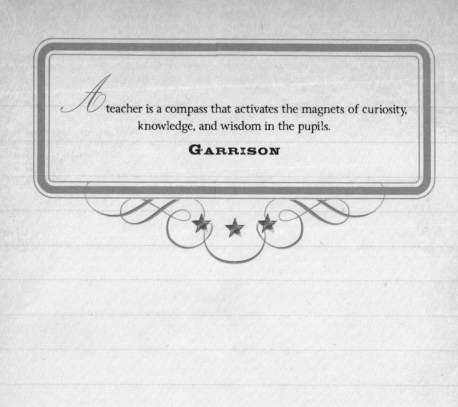

A teacher is a compass that activates the magnets of curiosity, knowledge, and wisdom in the pupils.

GARRISON

*G*ood leaders cultivate honest speech;
they love advisors who tell them the truth.

PROVERBS 16:13 THE MESSAGE

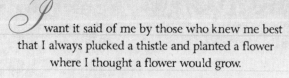

I want it said of me by those who knew me best that I always plucked a thistle and planted a flower where I thought a flower would grow.

ABRAHAM LINCOLN

The wisdom that comes from God is first of all pure, then peaceful, gentle, and easy to please. This wisdom is always ready to help.... People who work for peace in a peaceful way plant a good crop of right-living.

JAMES 3:17-18 NCV

Kind words are jewels that live in the heart and soul and remain as blessed memories years after they have been spoken.

MARVEA JOHNSON

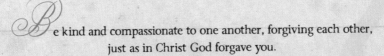

e kind and compassionate to one another, forgiving each other,
just as in Christ God forgave you.

EPHESIANS 4:32 NIV

Next in importance to Freedom and Justice is popular education, without which neither Freedom nor Justice can be permanently maintained.

JAMES A. GARFIELD

*A*lways remember what you have been taught, and don't let go of it.
Keep all that you have learned; it is the most important thing in life.

PROVERBS 4:13 NCV

Whatever you do, put romance and enthusiasm into the lives of our children.

MARGARET R. MACDONALD

Be an example to them by doing good works of every kind.
Let everything you do reflect the integrity and seriousness of your teaching.

TITUS 2:7 NLT

$\mathcal{T}$eachers believe they have a gift for giving; it drives them with the same irrepressible drive that drives others to create a work of art or a market or a building.

A. BARTLETT GIAMATTI

*Give generously...without a grudging heart, then because of this
the Lord your God will bless you in all your work and
in everything you put your hand to.*

DEUTERONOMY 15:10 NIV

It's a thrill to fulfill your own childhood dreams, but as you get older you may find that enabling the dreams of others is even more fun.

RANDY PAUSCH

*T*herefore encourage one another and build each other up,
just as in fact you are doing.

1 Thessalonians 5:11 niv

$\mathcal{G}$reat works do not always lie our way, but every moment we may do little ones excellently, that is, with great love.

FRANÇOIS DE SALES

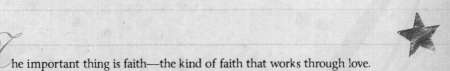

The important thing is faith—the kind of faith that works through love.

GALATIANS 5:6 NCV

Teachers do not plant seeds of curiosity
in the soil of young minds; the seeds are already there.
It is with care and nurturing that a teacher encourages
those seeds to sprout and grow and become a life of their own.

*M*ay the Lord make your love for one another
and for all people grow and overflow.

1 THESSALONIANS 3:12 NLT

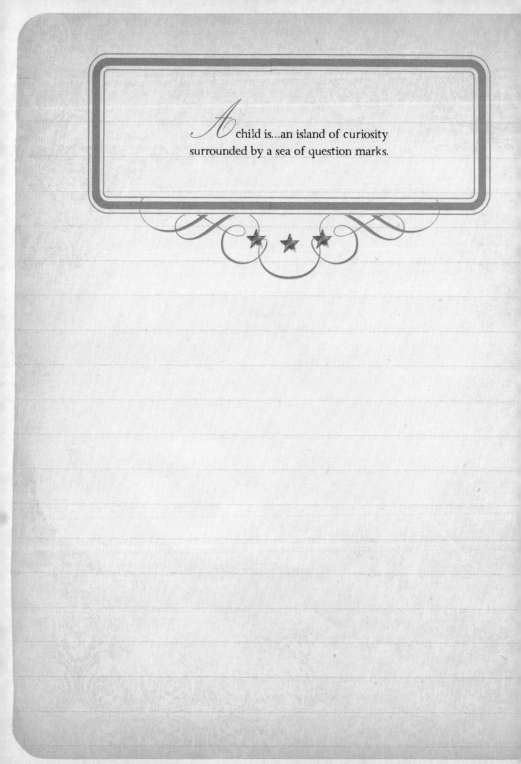

A child is...an island of curiosity
surrounded by a sea of question marks.

*O*God, You have taught me from my earliest childhood,
and I constantly tell others about the wonderful things You do.

PSALM 71:17 NLT

The role of the teacher remains the highest calling of a free people.
To the teacher, America entrusts her most precious resource,
her children, and asks that they be prepared...to face the rigors
of individual participation in a democratic society.

SHIRLEY MOUNT HUFSTEDLER

*W*e have different gifts, according to the grace given us.
If a man's gift is...serving, let him serve; if it is teaching, let him teach;
if it is encouraging, let him encourage.

ROMANS 12:6-8 NIV

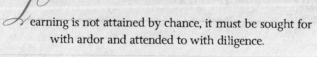

*L*earning is not attained by chance, it must be sought for
with ardor and attended to with diligence.

ABIGAIL ADAMS

Do not neglect your gift.... Be diligent in these matters;
give yourself wholly to them, so that everyone may see your progress.

1 TIMOTHY 4:14-15 NIV

$\mathcal{M}$y teacher, how can I ever thank you enough? What you have given me will stay with me a lifetime. Thank you for believing in me, for teaching me with patience and understanding.

CATHERINE PULSIFER

I thank my God upon every remembrance of you,
always in every prayer of mine making request for you all with joy.

PHILIPPIANS 1:3-4 NKJV

The true purpose of education is to cherish and unfold the seed of immortality already sown within us; to develop, to their fullest extent, the capacities of every kind with which the God who made us has endowed us.

ANNA JAMES

$\mathcal{W}$e should make the most of what God gives, both the bounty
and the capacity to enjoy it, accepting what's given and delighting in the work.
It's God's gift!

ECCLESIASTES 5:19 THE MESSAGE

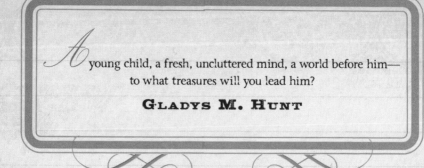

A young child, a fresh, uncluttered mind, a world before him—
to what treasures will you lead him?

GLADYS M. HUNT

The wolf also shall dwell with the lamb, the leopard shall lie down
with the young goat, the calf and the young lion and the fatling together;
and a little child shall lead them.

ISAIAH 11:6 NKJV

*L*ord...give me the gift of faith to be renewed and shared with others each day. Teach me to live this moment only, looking neither to the past with regret, nor the future with apprehension. Let love be my aim and my life a prayer.

ROSEANN ALEXANDER-ISHAM

If you have any encouragement from being united with Christ, if any comfort from His love,...then make my joy complete by being like-minded, having the same love, being one in spirit and purpose.

PHILIPPIANS 2:1-2 NIV

The supreme end of education is expert discernment in all things—
the power to tell the good from the bad,
the genuine from the counterfeit, and to prefer
the good and the genuine to the bad and the counterfeit.

SAMUEL JOHNSON

Pay attention to my wisdom; listen carefully to my wise counsel.
Then you will show discernment, and your lips will express what you've learned.

PROVERBS 5:1-2 NLT

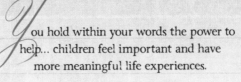

ou hold within your words the power to help... children feel important and have more meaningful life experiences.

DOUG FIELDS

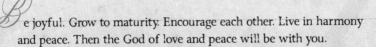

Be joyful. Grow to maturity. Encourage each other. Live in harmony and peace. Then the God of love and peace will be with you.

2 CORINTHIANS 13:11 NLT

Thank you for...making a difference, never giving up on anybody, respecting others, striving for excellence...not perfection, smiling a lot, never depriving our children of hope, keeping your promises, being a child's hero, giving your heart.

I thank God because in Christ you have been made rich in every way, in all your speaking and in all your knowledge.

1 CORINTHIANS 1:5 NCV

Books, study guides, chalkboard explanations and technology-enhanced analysis—all excellent tools to cultivate the intellect; but critical to the development of a student is the life, the warmth, the presence of a teacher.

*W*hatever you have learned or received or heard from me, or seen in me—
put it into practice. And the God of peace will be with you.

PHILIPPIANS 4:9 NIV

As teachers we use our initiative, our teaching skills, our spiritual and moral values, our creative abilities, our intellect and everything that we can muster to develop each child to his potential.

MARGARET PERRY TEUFEL

Do you see people skilled in their work?
They will work for kings, not for ordinary people.

PROVERBS 22:29 NCV

Each one of us is God's special work of art.
Through us, He teaches and inspires...those who view our lives.

JONI EARECKSON TADA

For we are God's workmanship, created in Christ Jesus to do good works,
which God prepared in advance for us to do.

EPHESIANS 2:10 NIV

My heart is singing for joy this morning. A miracle has happened! The light of understanding has shone upon my little pupil's mind, and behold, all things are changed!

ANNIE SULLIVAN

The entrance of Your words gives light;
It gives understanding to the simple.

PSALM 119:130 NKJV

Do more than exist; live.... Do more than look; observe....
Do more than hear; listen.... Do more than listen; understand.

JOHN H. RHOADES

*S*teep your life in God-reality, God-initiative, God-provisions.
Don't worry about missing out. You'll find
all your everyday human concerns will be met.

MATTHEW 6:33 THE MESSAGE

That energy which makes a child hard to manage is the energy which afterward makes him a manager of life.

HENRY WARD BEECHER

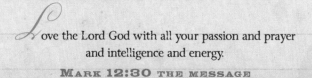

*L*ove the Lord God with all your passion and prayer
and intelligence and energy.

MARK 12:30 THE MESSAGE

A simple compliment may not alter a student's behavior immediately. But it does help get things moving in the right direction.

A. P. WITHAM

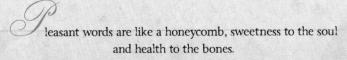

Pleasant words are like a honeycomb, sweetness to the soul
and health to the bones.

PROVERBS 16:24 NKJV

The place where God calls you to is the place
where your deep gladness and the world's deep hunger meet.

FREDERICK BUECHNER

He has given us everything we need to live and to serve God. We have these things because we know Him. Jesus called us by His glory and goodness.... With these gifts you can share in God's nature.

2 PETER 1:3-4 NCV

To open the minds and spirits of our young people we must help them feel love for the search for knowledge—a search to know the what and the why, to understand the hearts and minds of others, and to understand the meaning of the world and our place in it.

MARILYN JACHETTI WHIRRY

I f you receive my words, and treasure my commands within you, so that you incline your ear to wisdom, and apply your heart to understanding... then you will understand the fear of the Lord, and find the knowledge of God.

PROVERBS 2:1-2, 5 NKJV

*W*hether we are poets or parents or teachers or artists or gardeners, we must start where we are and use what we have.... What seems mundane and trivial may show itself to be a holy, precious, part of a pattern.

LUCI SHAW

*W*ell done, good and faithful servant! You have been faithful
with a few things; I will put you in charge of many things.
Come and share your master's happiness!

MATTHEW 25:23 NIV

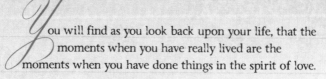

You ou will find as you look back upon your life, that the moments when you have really lived are the moments when you have done things in the spirit of love.

HENRY DRUMMOND

*H*ope does not disappoint, because the love of God
has been poured out in our hearts by the Holy Spirit who was given to us.

ROMANS 5:5 NKJV

To acquire knowledge, one must study;
but to acquire wisdom, one must observe.

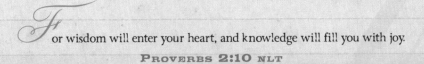

For wisdom will enter your heart, and knowledge will fill you with joy.

PROVERBS 2:10 NLT

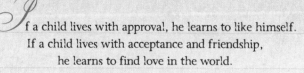

*f a child lives with approval, he learns to like himself.
If a child lives with acceptance and friendship,
he learns to find love in the world.*

DOROTHY LAW NOLTE

*L*et the little children come to Me, and do not forbid them;
for of such is the kingdom of heaven.

MATTHEW 19:14 NKJV

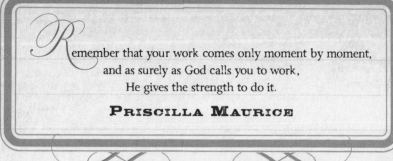

Remember that your work comes only moment by moment,
and as surely as God calls you to work,
He gives the strength to do it.

PRISCILLA MAURICE

The Lord is my strength and my shield; my heart trusted in Him,
and I am helped; therefore my heart greatly rejoices,
and with my song I will praise Him.

PSALM 28:7 NKJV

One of the most important things a teacher can do is to send the pupil home in the afternoon liking himself just a little better than when he came in the morning.

ERNEST MELBY

*W*e can't help but thank God for you, because your faith
is flourishing and your love for one another is growing.

2 THESSALONIANS 1:3 NLT

A student never forgets an encouraging private word, when it is given with sincere respect and admiration.

WILLIAM LYON PHELPS

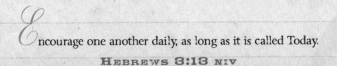
*E*ncourage one another daily, as long as it is called Today.

HEBREWS 3:13 NIV

$\mathcal{E}$arth and sky, woods and fields, lakes and rivers, the mountain and the sea, are excellent schoolmasters, and teach some of us more than we can ever learn from books.

SIR JOHN LUBBOCK

*G*od sets out the entire creation as a science classroom,
using birds and beasts to teach wisdom.

JOB 35:11 THE MESSAGE

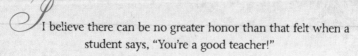

I believe there can be no greater honor than that felt when a student says, "You're a good teacher!"

THOMAS A. FLEMING

The wise are known for their understanding.
Their pleasant words make them better teachers.

PROVERBS 16:21 NCV

The dream begins with a teacher who believes in you, who tugs and pushes and leads you to the next plateau, sometimes poking you with a sharp stick called "truth."

DAN RATHER

*F*ix your thoughts on what is true, and honorable,
and right, and pure, and lovely, and admirable.
Think about things that are excellent and worthy of praise.

PHILIPPIANS 4:8 NLT

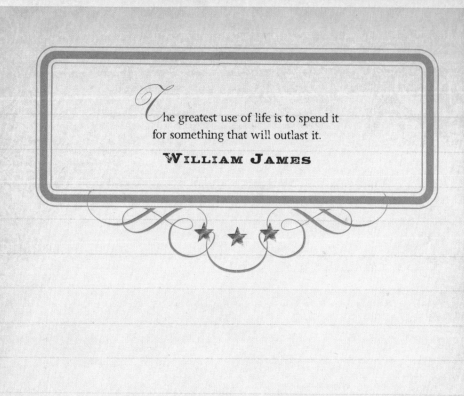

The greatest use of life is to spend it
for something that will outlast it.

WILLIAM JAMES

*L*et us not get tired of doing what is right,
for after a while we will reap a harvest of blessing.

GALATIANS 6:9 TLB

The task of the excellent teacher is to stimulate "apparently ordinary" people to unusual effort. The tough problem is not in identifying winners: it is in making winners out of ordinary people.

K. PATRICIA CROSS

*L*ove and truth form a good leader;
sound leadership is founded on loving integrity.

PROVERBS 20:28 THE MESSAGE

Genuine appreciation of other people's children
is one of the rarer virtues.

*L*ove each other with genuine affection,
and take delight in honoring each other.

ROMANS 12:10 NLT

It is important that students bring a certain ragamuffin, barefoot irreverence to their studies; they are not here to worship what is known, but to question it.

JACOB BRONOWSKI

The heart of the discerning acquires knowledge;
the ears of the wise seek it out.

PROVERBS 18:15 NIV

Do all the good you can by all the means you can in all the ways you can in all the places you can to all the people you can as long as ever you can.

JOHN WESLEY

*W*ork with enthusiasm, as though you were
working for the Lord rather than for people.

EPHESIANS 6:7 NLT

*H*aving an abundance of information committed to memory
makes no difference to the world compared to the effect
of one who has the ability to put a speck of knowledge
into action and affect the greater good.

Understanding is like a fountain which gives life to those who use it.

PROVERBS 16:22 NCV

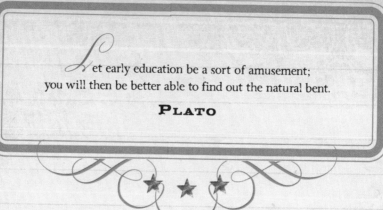

*Let early education be a sort of amusement;
you will then be better able to find out the natural bent.*

PLATO

*rain up a child in the way he should go,
and when he is old he will not depart from it.

PROVERBS 22:6 NKJV

When I approach a child, he inspires in me two sentiments: tenderness for what he is, and respect for what he may become.

LOUIS PASTEUR

*Nothing could make me happier than getting reports
that my children continue diligently in the way of Truth!*

3 JOHN 1:4 THE MESSAGE

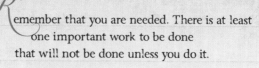

Remember that you are needed. There is at least one important work to be done that will not be done unless you do it.

CHARLES L. ALLEN

To enjoy your work and to accept your lot in life—
that is indeed a gift from God. The person who does that
will not need to look back with sorrow on his past, for God gives him joy.

ECCLESIASTES 5:20 TLB

You have a special way of caring and bringing out the best in all your students. Thanks for daring to believe the best of us.